MANUAL OF THE WARRIOR OF LIGHT

MANUAL OF THE WARRIOR OF LIGHT

Paulo Coelho

Translated from the Portuguese by
Margaret Jull Costa

CHIVERS

British Library Cataloguing in Publication Data available

This Large Print edition published by BBC Audiobooks Ltd, Bath, 2005.
Published by arrangement with HarperCollins Publishers Ltd.

U.K. Hardcover ISBN 1 4056 3146 5
U.K. Softcover ISBN 1 4056 3147 3

Printed and bound in Great Britain by

Hail Mary conceived without sin, pray for those who turn to you. Amen.

For S.I.L., Carlos Eduardo Rangel and Anne Carrière, masters of rigour and compassion.

AUTHOR'S NOTE

With the exception of the prologue and the epilogue, the material contained in this book was first published in a column entitled 'Maktub', which appeared in Folha de São Paulo between 1993 and 1996 as well as in various other newspapers in Brazil and elsewhere.

The disciple is not above his master; but every one that is perfect shall be as his master.

LUKE 6:40

PROLOGUE

'Just off the beach to the west of the village lies an island, and on it is a vast temple with many bells,' said the woman.

The boy noticed that she was dressed strangely and had a veil covering her head. He had never seen her before.

'Have you ever visited that temple?' she asked. 'Go there and tell me what you think of it?'

Seduced by the woman's beauty, the boy went to the place she had indicated. He sat down on the beach and stared out at the horizon, but he saw only what he always saw: blue sky and ocean.

Disappointed, he walked to a nearby fishing village and asked if anyone there knew about an island and a temple.

'Oh, that was many years ago, when my great-grandparents were alive,' said an old fisherman. 'There was an earthquake, and the island was swallowed up by the sea. But although we can no longer see the island, we can still hear the temple bells when the ocean sets them swinging down below.'

The boy went back to the beach and tried to hear the bells. He spent the whole afternoon there, but all he heard was the noise of the waves and the cries of the seagulls.

When night fell, his parents came looking for him. The following morning, he went back to the beach; he could not believe that such a beautiful woman would have lied to him. If she ever returned, he could tell her that, although he had not seen the island, he had heard the temple bells set ringing by the motion of the waves.

Many months passed; the woman did not return and the boy forgot all about her; now he was convinced that he needed to discover the riches and treasures in the submerged temple. If he could hear the bells, he would be able to locate it and salvage the treasure hidden below.

He lost interest in school and even in his friends. He became the butt of all the other children's jokes. They used to say: 'He's not like us. He prefers to sit looking at the sea because he's afraid of being beaten in our games.'

And they all laughed to see the boy sitting on the shore.

Although he still could not hear the old temple

bells ringing, the boy learned about other things. He began to realise that he had grown so used to the sound of the waves that he was no longer distracted by them. Soon after that, he became used to the cries of the seagulls, the buzzing of the bees and the wind blowing amongst the palm trees.

Six months after his first conversation with the woman, the boy could sit there oblivious to all other noises, but he still could not hear the bells from the drowned temple.

Fishermen came and talked to him, insisting that they had heard the bells.

But the boy never did.

Some time later, however, the fishermen changed their tune: 'You spend far too much time thinking about the bells beneath the sea. Forget about them and go back to playing with your friends. Perhaps it's only fishermen who can hear them.'

After almost a year, the boy thought: 'Perhaps they're right. I would do better to grow up and become a fisherman and come down to this beach every morning, because I've come to love it here.' And he thought too: 'Perhaps it's just another legend and the bells were all shattered during the earthquake and have never rung out since.'

That afternoon, he decided to go back home.

He walked down to the ocean to say goodbye. He looked once more at the natural world around him and because he was no longer concerned about the bells, he could again smile at the beauty of the seagulls' cries, the roar of the sea and the wind blowing in the palm trees. Far off, he heard the sound of his friends playing and he felt glad to think that he would soon resume his childhood games.

The boy was happy and—as only a child can— he felt grateful for being alive. He was sure that he had not wasted his time, for he had learned to contemplate Nature and to respect it.

Then, because he was listening to the sea, the seagulls, the wind in the palm trees and the voices of his friends playing, he also heard the first bell.

And then another.

And another, until, to his great joy, all the bells in the drowned temple were ringing.

Years later, when he was a grown man, he returned to the village and to the beach of his childhood. He no longer dreamed of finding treasure at the bottom of the sea; perhaps that had all been a product of his imagination, and he had never really heard the submerged bells ring out on one lost childhood afternoon. Even so, he decided to walk for a while along the beach, to listen to the noise of the wind and to the cries of the seagulls.

Imagine his surprise when, there on the beach, he saw the woman who had first spoken to him about the island and its temple.

'What are you doing here?' he asked.

'I was waiting for you,' she replied.

He noticed that, despite the passing years, the woman looked exactly the same; the veil hiding her hair had not faded with time.

She handed him a blue notebook full of blank pages.

'Write: a warrior of light values a child's eyes because they are able to look at the world without bitterness. When he wants to find out if the person beside him is worthy of his trust, he tries to see him as a child would.'

'What is a warrior of light?'

'You already know that,' she replied with a smile. 'He is someone capable of understanding the miracle of life, of fighting to the last for something he believes in—and of hearing the bells that the waves sets ringing on

xiii

the seabed.'

He had never thought of himself as a warrior of light. The woman seemed to read his thoughts. 'Everyone is capable of these things. And, though no one thinks of themselves as a warrior of light, we all are.'

He looked at the blank pages in the notebook. The woman smiled again.

'Write about that warrior,' she said.

A warrior of light knows that he has much to be grateful for.

He was helped in his struggle by the angels; celestial forces placed each thing in its place, thus allowing him to give of his best.

His companions say: 'He's so lucky!' And the warrior does sometimes achieve things far beyond his capabilities.

That is why, at sunset, he kneels and gives thanks for the Protective Cloak surrounding him.

His gratitude, however, is not limited to the spiritual world; he never forgets his friends, for their blood mingled with his on the battlefield.

A warrior does not need to be reminded of the help given him by others; he is the first to remember and he makes sure to share with them any rewards he receives.

All the world's roads lead to the heart of the warrior; he plunges unhesitatingly into the river of passions always flowing through his life.

The warrior knows that he is free to choose his desires, and he makes these decisions with courage, detachment and—sometimes—with just a touch of madness.

He embraces his passions and enjoys them intensely. He knows that there is no need to renounce the pleasures of conquest; they are part of life and bring joy to all those who participate in them.

But he never loses sight of those things that last or of the strong bonds that are forged over time.

A warrior can distinguish between the transient and the enduring.

A warrior of light does not rely on strength alone, he makes use of his opponent's energy too.

When he enters the fight, all he has is his enthusiasm and the moves and strikes that he learned during his training. As the fight progresses, he discovers that enthusiasm and training are not enough to win: what counts is experience.

Then he opens his heart to the Universe and asks God to give him the inspiration he needs to turn every blow from his enemy into a lesson in self-defence.

His companions say: 'He's so superstitious. He stopped fighting in order to pray; he even shows respect for his opponent's tricks.'

The warrior does not respond to these provocations. He knows that without inspiration and experience, no amount of training will help him.

A warrior of light never resorts to trickery, but he knows how to distract his opponent.

However anxious he is, he uses every strategy at his disposal to gain his objective. When he sees that his strength is almost gone, he makes his enemy think that he is simply biding his time. When he needs to attack the right flank, he moves his troops to the left. If he intends beginning the battle at once, he pretends that he is tired and prepares for sleep.

His friends say: 'Look, he's lost all enthusiasm.' But he pays no attention to such remarks because his friends do not understand his tactics.

A warrior of light knows what he wants. And he has no need to waste time on explanations.

A wise Chinese man has this to say about the strategies of the warrior of light:

'Convince your enemy that he will gain very little by attacking you; this will diminish his enthusiasm.'

'Do not be ashamed to make a temporary withdrawal from the field if you see that your enemy is stronger than you; it is not winning or losing a single battle that matters, but how the war ends.'

'Even if you are very strong, never be ashamed to feign weakness; this will make your enemy act imprudently and attack too soon.'

'In war, the key to victory is the ability to surprise one's opponent.'

'It's odd,' says the warrior of light to himself. 'I have met so many people who, at the first opportunity, try to show their very worst qualities. They hide their inner strength behind aggression; they hide their fear of loneliness behind an air of independence. They do not believe in their own abilities, but are constantly trumpeting their virtues.'

The warrior reads these messages in many of the men and women he meets. He is never taken in by appearances and makes a point of remaining silent when people try to impress him. And he uses the occasion to correct his own faults, for other people make an excellent mirror.

A warrior takes every opportunity to teach himself.

The warrior of light sometimes fights with those he loves.

The man who defends his friends is never overwhelmed by the storms of life; he is strong enough to come through difficulties and to carry on.

However, he is often faced by challenges from those he is trying to teach the art of the sword. His disciples provoke him into fighting with them.

And the warrior demonstrates his abilities: with just a few blows he disarms his students, and harmony returns to the place where they meet.

'Why bother to do that, when you are so much better than they are?' asks a traveller.

'Because in challenging me, what they really want is to talk to me and this is my way of keeping the dialogue open,' replies the warrior.

Before embarking on an important battle, a warrior of light asks himself: 'How far have I developed my abilities?'

He knows that he has learned something with every battle he has fought, but many of those lessons have caused him unnecessary suffering. More than once he has wasted his time fighting for a lie. And he has suffered for people who did not deserve his love.

Victors never make the same mistake twice. That is why the warrior only risks his heart for something worthwhile.

A warrior of light respects the main teaching of the *I Ching:* 'To persevere is favourable.'

He knows that perseverance is not the same thing as insistence. There are times when battles go on longer than necessary, draining him of strength and enthusiasm.

At such moments, the warrior thinks: 'A prolonged war finally destroys the victors too.'

Then he withdraws his forces from the battlefield and allows himself a respite. He perseveres in his desire, but knows he must wait for the best moment to attack.

A warrior always returns to the fray. He never does so out of stubbornness, but because he has noticed a change in the weather.

A warrior of light knows that certain moments repeat themselves.

He often finds himself faced by the same problems and situations, and seeing these difficult situations return, he grows depressed, thinking that he is incapable of making any progress in life.

'I've been through all this before,' he says to his heart.

'Yes, you have been through all this before,' replies his heart. 'But you have never been beyond it.'

Then the warrior realises that these repeated experiences have but one aim: to teach him what he does not want to learn.

A warrior of light is never predictable.

He might dance down the street on his way to work, gaze into the eyes of a complete stranger and speak of love at first sight, or defend an apparently absurd idea. Warriors of light allow themselves days like these.

He is not afraid to weep over ancient sorrows or feel joy at new discoveries. When he feels that the moment has arrived, he drops everything and goes off on some long-dreamed-of adventure. When he realises that he can do no more, he abandons the fight, but never blames himself for having committed a few unexpected acts of folly.

A warrior does not spend his days trying to play the role that others have chosen for him.

Warriors of light always have a certain gleam in their eyes.

They are of this world, they are part of the lives of other people and they set out on their journey with no saddlebags and no sandals. They are often cowardly. They do not always make the right decisions.

They suffer over the most trivial things, they have mean thoughts and sometimes believe they are incapable of growing. They frequently deem themselves unworthy of any blessing or miracle.

They are not always quite sure what they are doing here. They spend many sleepless nights, believing that their lives have no meaning.

That is why they are warriors of light. Because they make mistakes. Because they ask themselves questions. Because they are looking for a reason—and are sure to find it.

The warrior of light does not worry that, to others, his behaviour might seem quite mad.

He talks out loud to himself when he is alone. Someone told him that this is the best way of communicating with the angels, and so he takes a chance and tries to make contact.

At first, he finds this very difficult. He thinks that he has nothing to say, that he will just repeat the same meaningless twaddle. Even so, the warrior persists. He spends all day talking to his heart. He says things with which he does not agree, he talks utter nonsense.

One day, he notices a change in his voice. He realises that he is acting as a channel for some higher wisdom.

The warrior may seem mad, but this is just a disguise.

According to a poet: 'The warrior of light chooses his enemies.'

He knows what he is capable of; he does not have to go about the world boasting of his qualities and virtues. Nevertheless, there is always someone who wants to prove himself better than he is.

For the warrior, there is no 'better' or 'worse': everyone has the necessary gifts for his particular path.

But certain people insist. They provoke and offend and do everything they can to irritate him. At that point, his heart says: 'Do not respond to these insults, they will not increase your abilities. You will tire yourself needlessly.'

A warrior of light does not waste his time listening to provocations; he has a destiny to fulfil.

The warrior of light remembers a passage from John Bunyan:

'Although I have been through all that I have, I do not regret the many hardships I met, because it was they who brought me to the place I wished to reach. Now all I have is this sword and I give it to whomever wishes to continue his pilgrimage. I carry with me the marks and scars of battles—they are the witnesses of what I suffered and the rewards of what I conquered.

'These are the beloved marks and scars that will open the gates of Paradise to me. There was a time when I used to listen to tales of bravery. There was a time when I lived only because I needed to live. But now I live because I am a warrior and because I wish one day to be in the company of Him for whom I have fought so hard.'

The moment that he begins to walk along it, the warrior of light recognises the Path.

Each stone, each bend cries welcome to him. He identifies with the mountains and the streams, he sees something of his own soul in the plants and the animals and the birds of the field.

Then, accepting the help of God and of God's Signs, he allows his Personal Legend to guide him towards the tasks that life has reserved for him.

On some nights, he has nowhere to sleep, on others, he suffers from insomnia. 'That's just how it is,' thinks the warrior. 'I was the one who chose to walk this path.'

In these words lies all his power: he chose the path along which he is walking and so has no complaints.

From now on—and for the next few hundred years—the Universe is going to help warriors of light and hinder the prejudiced.

The Earth's energy needs to be renewed.

New ideas need space.

Body and soul need new challenges.

The future has become the present, and every dream—except those dreams that involve preconceived ideas—will have a chance to be heard.

Anything of importance will remain; anything useless will disappear. However, it is not the warrior's responsibility to judge the dreams of others, and he does not waste time criticising other people's decisions.

In order to have faith in his own path, he does not need to prove that someone else's path is wrong.

A warrior of light carefully studies the position that he intends to conquer.

However difficult the objective, there is always a way of overcoming obstacles. He seeks out alternative paths, he sharpens his sword, he tries to fill his heart with the necessary determination to face the challenge.

But as he advances, the warrior realises that there are difficulties he had not reckoned with.

If he waits for the ideal moment, he will never set off; he requires a touch of madness to take the next step.

The warrior uses that touch of madness. For—in both love and war—it is impossible to foresee everything.

A warrior of light knows his own faults. But he also knows his qualities.

Some of his companions complain all the time that 'other people have more opportunities than we do'.

Perhaps they are right, but a warrior does not allow himself to be paralysed by this; he tries to make the most of his virtues.

He knows that the gazelle's power lies in its strong legs. The power of the seagull lies in the accuracy with which it can spear a fish. He has learned that the reason the tiger does not fear the hyena is because he is aware of his own strength.

He tries to establish what he can truly rely on. And he always checks that he carries three things with him: faith, hope and love.

If these three things are there, he does not hesitate to go forward.

The warrior of light knows that no one is stupid and that life teaches everyone—however long that may take.

He always does his best and expects the best of others.Through his generosity, he tries to show each person how much they are capable of achieving.

Some of his companions say: 'Some people are so ungrateful.'

The warrior is not discouraged by this. And he continues to encourage other people because this is also a way of encouraging himself.

Every warrior of light has trodden a path that was not his.

Every warrior of light has suffered for the most trivial of reasons.

Every warrior of light has, at least once, believed that he was not a warrior of light.

Every warrior of light has failed in his spiritual duties.

Every warrior of light has said 'yes' when he wanted to say 'no'.

Every warrior of light has hurt someone he loved.

That is why he is a warrior of light, because he has been through all this and yet has never lost hope of being better than he is.

The warrior always listens to the words of certain thinkers, such as these by T.H. Huxley:

'The consequences of our actions are the scarecrows of fools and the beacons of wise men.'

'The chessboard is the world; the pieces are the gestures of our daily lives; the rules of the game are what we call the laws of Nature. The player on the other side is hidden from us, but we know that his play is always fair, just and patient.'

The warrior simply has to accept the challenge. He knows that God never overlooks a single mistake made by those he loves, nor does he allow his favourites to pretend ignorance of the rules of the game.

Awarrior of light does not postpone making decisions.

He thinks a good deal before he acts; he considers his training, as well as his responsibilities and duties as a teacher. He tries to remain calm and to analyse each step as if it were of supreme importance.

However, as soon as he has made a decision, the warrior proceeds: he has no doubts about his chosen action, nor does he change direction if circumstances turn out differently from how he had imagined them.

If his decision is correct, he will win the battle, even if it lasts longer than expected. If his decision is wrong, he will be defeated and he will have to start all over again—only this time with more wisdom.

But once he has started, a warrior of light perseveres until the end.

A warrior knows that his best teachers are the people with whom he shares the battlefield.

It is dangerous to ask for advice. It is even more dangerous to give advice. When he needs help, he tries to see how his friends resolve—or fail, to resolve—their problems.

If he is in search of inspiration, he reads on the lips of his neighbour the words that his guardian angel is trying to say to him.

When he is tired or lonely, he does not dream about distant men and women; he turns to the person beside him and shares his sorrow or his need for affection with them—with pleasure and without guilt.

A warrior knows that the farthest-flung star in the Universe reveals itself in the things around him.

A warrior of light shares his world with the people he loves.

He tries to encourage them to do the things they would like to do but for which they lack the courage; at such times, the Enemy appears holding two wooden signs in his hand.

On one sign is written: 'Think about yourself. Keep all the blessings for yourself, otherwise you'll end up losing everything.'

On the other sign, he reads: Who do you think you are, helping other people? Can't you see your own faults?'

A warrior knows that he has faults. But he knows too that he cannot do his growing alone and thus distance himself from his companions.

Therefore, he throws the two signs to the floor, even if he thinks they may contain a grain of truth. The signs crumble into dust, and the warrior continues to encourage those nearest him.

The philosopher Lao Tzu says of the journey of the warrior of light:

'The Way involves respect for all small and subtle things. Learn to recognise the right moment to adopt the necessary attitudes.'

'Even if you have already fired a bow several times, continue to pay attention to how you position the arrow and how you flex the string.'

'When a beginner knows what he needs, he proves more intelligent than an absent-minded sage.'

'Accumulating love brings luck, accumulating hatred brings calamity. Anyone who fails to recognise problems leaves the door open for tragedies to rush in.'

'The battle is not the same as the quarrel.'

The warrior of light meditates.

He sits in a quiet place in his tent and surrenders himself to the divine light. When he does this, he tries not to think about anything; he shuts himself off from the search for pleasure, from challenges and revelations, and allows his gifts and powers to reveal themselves.

Even if he does not recognise them then, these gifts and powers are taking care of his life and will influence his day-to-day existence.

While he meditates, the warrior is not himself, but a spark from the Soul of the World. These are the moments that give him an understanding of his responsibilities and of how he should behave accordingly.

A warrior of light knows that in the silence of his heart he will hear an order that will guide him.

'When I draw my bow,' says Herrigel to his Zen master, 'there comes a point when I feel as if I will get breathless if I do not let fly at once.'

'If you continue to try to provoke the moment when you must release the arrow, you will never learn the art of the archer,' says his master. 'Sometimes, it is the archer's own overactive desire that ruins the accuracy of the shot.'

A warrior of light sometimes thinks: 'If I do not do something, it will not be done.'

It is not quite like that: he must act, but he must allow room for the Universe to act too.

When a warrior is the victim of some injustice, he usually tries to be alone, in order not to show his pain to others.

This is both good and bad.

It is one thing to allow one's heart to heal its wounds slowly, but it is quite another to sit all day in deep contemplation for fear of seeming weak.

Inside each of us there lives an angel and a devil, and their voices are very alike. Confronted by a problem, the devil encourages that solitary conversation, trying to show us how vulnerable we are. The angel makes us reflect upon our attitudes and occasionally needs someone else's mouth to reveal itself.

A warrior balances solitude and dependence.

A warrior of light needs love.

Love and affection are as much a part of his nature as eating and drinking and a taste for the Good Fight. When the warrior watches a sunset and feels no joy, then something is wrong.

At this point, he stops fighting and goes in search of company, so that they can watch the setting sun together.

If he has difficulty in finding company, he asks himself: 'Was I too afraid to approach someone? Did I receive affection and not even notice?'

A warrior of light makes use of solitude, but is not used by it.

.

The warrior of light knows that it is impossible to live in a state of complete relaxation.

He has learned from the archer that, in order to shoot his arrow any distance, he must hold the bow taut. He has learned from the stars that only an inner explosion allows them to shine. The warrior notices that when a horse is about to jump over a fence, it tenses all its muscles.

But he never confuses tension with anxiety.

The warrior of light always manages to balance Rigour and Mercy.

To attain his dream, he needs a strong will and an enormous capacity for acceptance; although he may have an objective, the path that leads to that objective is not always as he imagined it would be.

That is why the warrior uses a mixture of discipline and compassion. God never abandons His children, but His purposes are unfathomable, and He builds the road with our own steps.

The warrior uses that combination of discipline and acceptance to fuel his enthusiasm. Routine was never at the head of any important new movement.

The warrior of light sometimes behaves like water, flowing around the obstacles he encounters.

Occasionally, resisting might mean being destroyed, and so he adapts to the circumstances. He accepts without complaint that the stones along the path hinder his way across the mountains.

Therein lies the strength of water: it cannot be shattered by a hammer or wounded by a knife. The strongest sword in the world cannot scar its surface.

The waters of a river adapt themselves to whatever route proves possible, but the river never forgets its one objective: the sea. So fragile at its source, it gradually gathers the strength of the other rivers it encounters.

And, after a certain point, its power is absolute.

For the warrior of light, there are no abstractions.

Everything is concrete and everything is meaningful. He does not sit comfortably in his tent, observing what is going on in the world; he accepts each challenge as an opportunity to transform himself.

Some of his companions spend their lives moaning about their lack of choice or passing comment on the decisions made by other people. The warrior, however, transforms his thinking into action.

Sometimes he chooses the wrong goal and pays the price for his mistake without complaint. At others, he swerves from the path and wastes a great deal of time only to end up back where he started.

But the warrior never allows himself to be discouraged.

The warrior of light has the qualities of a rock.

When he is on flat terrain, everything around him is in harmony and he remains stable. People can build their houses upon him, and the storm will not destroy them.

When, however, he is placed on a slope, and the things around him show neither balance nor respect, then he reveals his strength; he rolls towards the enemy that is threatening his peace. At such moments, the warrior is a devastating force, and no one can stop him.

A warrior of light thinks about both war and peace and knows how to act in accordance with the circumstances.

A warrior of light who trusts too much in his intelligence will end up underestimating the power of his opponent.

It is important not to forget that sometimes strength is more effective than strategy.

A bullfight lasts fifteen minutes; the bull quickly learns that it is being tricked, and its next step is to charge the bullfighter. When that happens, no amount of brilliance, argument, intelligence or charm can avert tragedy.

That is why the warrior never underestimates brute force. When it proves too violent, he withdraws from the battlefield until his enemy has exhausted himself.

The warrior of light knows when an enemy is stronger than he is.

If he decides to confront him, he will be destroyed instantly. If he responds to his provocations, he will fall into a trap. So he uses diplomacy to resolve the difficult situation in which he finds himself. When the enemy behaves like a baby, he does the same. When he challenges him to a fight, he pretends not to understand.

His friends say: 'He's a coward.'

But the warrior pays no attention; he knows that all the rage and courage of a little bird are as nothing to a cat.

In such situations, the warrior remains patient; the enemy will soon go off in search of others to provoke.

A warrior of light is never indifferent to injustice.

He knows that all is one and that each individual action affects everyone on the planet. That is why, when confronted by the suffering of others, he uses his sword to restore order.

But even though he fights against oppression, at no point does he attempt to judge the oppressor. Each person will answer for his actions before God and so, once the warrior has completed his task, he makes no further comment.

A warrior of light is in the world in order to help his fellow man, not to condemn his neighbour.

A warrior of light is never cowardly.

Flight might be an excellent form of defence, but it cannot be used when one is very afraid. When in doubt, the warrior prefers to face defeat and then lick his wounds, because he knows that if he flees he is giving to the aggressor greater power than he deserves.

In difficult and painful times, the warrior faces overwhelming odds with heroism, resignation and courage.

A warrior of light is never in a hurry.

Time works in his favour; he learns to master his impatience and avoids acting without thinking.

By walking slowly, he becomes aware of the firmness of his step. He knows that he is taking part in a decisive moment in the history of humanity and that he needs to change himself before he can transform the world. That is why he remembers the words of Lanza del Vasto: 'A revolution takes time to settle in.'

A warrior never picks fruit while it is still green.

A warrior of light needs both patience and speed.

The two worst strategic mistakes to make are acting prematurely and letting an opportunity slip; to avoid this, the warrior treats each situation as if it were unique and never resorts to formulae, recipes or other people's opinions.

The caliph Moauiyat asked Omr Ben Al-Aas the secret of his great political skills:

'I never get involved in something without having first worked out my retreat; then again, I have never gone into a situation and immediately wanted to run straight out again,' came the answer.

A warrior of light often loses heart.

He believes that nothing can stir in him the emotion he so desired. He is forced to spend many evenings and nights feeling that he is one of the vanquished, and nothing seems able to restore his enthusiasm.

His friends say: 'Perhaps his fight is over.'

The warrior feels pain and confusion when he hears such remarks because he knows that he has not yet reached the place he wanted to reach. But he is stubborn and refuses to relinquish his aims.

Then, when he least expects it, a new door opens.

A warrior of light always keeps his heart free of any feelings of hatred.

When he goes into battle, he remembers what Christ said: 'Love your enemies.' And he obeys.

But he knows that the act of forgiveness does not mean that he must accept everything; a warrior cannot bow his head, for if he did he would lose sight of the horizon of his dreams.

He accepts that his opponents are there to test his valour, his persistence, his ability to make decisions. They force him to fight for his dreams.

It is the experience of battle that strengthens the warrior of light.

The warrior remembers the past.

He knows about man's Spiritual Quest, he knows that this Quest has been responsible for some of history's finest pages.

But also some of history's worst chapters: massacres, sacrifices, obscurantism. It was used for personal ends and has seen its ideas used to defend the most terrible of intentions.

The warrior has heard people ask: 'How am I to know that the path I am on is the right path?' And he has seen many people abandon their quest because they could not answer that question.

The warrior has no doubts; he follows one infallible saying:

'By their fruits ye shall know them,' said Jesus. That is the rule he follows, and he never goes wrong.

The warrior of light knows the importance of intuition.

In the midst of battle, he does not have time to think about the enemy's blows, and so he uses his instinct and obeys his angel.

In times of peace, he deciphers the signs that God sends him.

People say: 'He's mad.'

Or: 'He lives in a fantasy world.'

Or even: 'How can he possibly believe in such illogical things?'

But the warrior knows that intuition is God's alphabet and he continues listening to the wind and talking to the stars.

The warrior of light sits around a fire with his companions.

They talk about his conquests, and any strangers who join the group are made welcome because everyone is proud of his life and of his Good Fight. The warrior speaks enthusiastically about the path, he tells how he resisted a particular challenge or speaks of the solution he found to one especially difficult situation. When he tells stories, he invests his words with passion and romance.

Sometimes, he exaggerates a little. He remembers that at times his ancestors used to exaggerate too.

That is why he does the same thing. But he never confuses pride with vanity, and he never believes his own exaggerations.

The warrior hears someone say: 'I need to understand everything before I can make a decision. I want to have the freedom to change my mind.'

The warrior regards these words suspiciously. He too can enjoy that freedom, but this does not prevent him from taking on a commitment, even if he does not know quite why he does so.

A warrior of light makes decisions. His soul is as free as the clouds in the sky, but he is committed to his dream. On his freely chosen path, he often has to get up earlier than he would like, speak to people from whom he learns nothing, make certain sacrifices.

His friends say: 'You're not free.'

The warrior is free. But he knows that an open oven bakes no bread.

To engage in any activity you need to know what you can expect, how to achieve your objective, and whether or not you are capable of carrying out the proposed task.

'Only a person who, suitably equipped, feels no desire for the results of conquest and yet remains absorbed in the struggle can truly say that he has renounced the fruits of victory.

One can renounce the fruit, but that renunciation does not signal indifference to the results.'

The warrior of light listens with respect to Gandhi's strategy. And he remains unconvinced by those who, incapable of achieving any result at all, preach renunciation.

The warrior of light pays attention to small things because they can severely hamper him.

A thorn, however tiny, can cause the traveller to halt. A tiny, invisible cell can destroy a healthy organism. The memory of a past moment of fear allows cowardice to be reborn with each new morning. A fraction of a second opens the way for the enemy's fatal blow.

The warrior is attentive to small things. Sometimes he is hard on himself, but he prefers to act in this way.

'The devil is in the detail,' says one of the Tradition's old proverbs.

The warrior of light does not always have faith.

There are moments when he believes in absolutely nothing. And he asks his heart: 'Is all this effort really worth it?'

But his heart remains silent. And the warrior has to decide for himself.

Then he looks for an example. And he remembers that Jesus went through something similar in order fully to inhabit the human condition.

'Take away this cup from me,' said Jesus. He too lost heart and courage, but he did not stop.

The warrior of light continues despite his lack of faith. He goes forward and, in the end, faith returns.

The warrior knows that no man is an island.

He cannot fight alone; whatever his plan, he depends on other people. He needs to discuss his strategy, to ask for help, and—in moments of relaxation—to have someone with whom he can sit by the fire, someone he can regale with tales of battle.

But he does not allow people to confuse this camaraderie with insecurity. He is transparent in his actions and secretive in his plans.

A warrior of light dances with his companions, but does not place the responsibility for his actions on anyone else.

In the intervals between battles, the warrior rests.

Often he spends whole days doing nothing, because that is what his heart demands; but his intuition remains alert. He does not commit the capital sin of Sloth, because he knows where that can lead—to the warm monotony of Sunday afternoons when time simply passes.

The warrior calls this 'the peace of the cemetery'. He remembers a passage from Revelation: 'I know thy works, that thou art neither cold nor hot . . . So then because thou art lukewarm and neither cold nor hot, I will spew thee out of my mouth.'

A warrior rests and laughs. But he is always alert.

The warrior of light knows that everyone is afraid of everyone else.

This fear generally manifests itself in two ways: through aggression or through submission. They are two facets of the same problem.

That is why, whenever he finds himself before someone who fills him with fear, the warrior reminds himself that the other person has the some insecurities as he has. He has surmounted similar obstacles and experienced the same problems.

But he knows how to deal with the situation better. Why? Because he uses fear as an engine, not as a brake.

The warrior learns from his opponent and acts in a like manner.

For the warrior there is no such thing as an impossible love.

He is not intimidated by silence, indifference or rejection. He knows that, behind the mask of ice that people wear, there beats a heart of fire.

This is why the warrior takes more risks than other people. He is constantly seeking the love of someone, even if that means often having to hear the word 'no', returning home defeated and feeling rejected in body and soul.

A warrior never gives in to fear when he is searching for what he needs. Without love, he is nothing.

The warrior of light recognises the silence that precedes an important battle.

And that silence seems to be saying: 'Things have stopped. Why not forget about fighting and enjoy yourself a little.' At this point, inexperienced combatants lay down their arms and complain that they are bored.

The warrior listens intently to that silence; somewhere something is happening. He knows that devastating earthquakes arrive without warning. He has walked through forests at night and knows that it is precisely when the animals are silent that danger is near.

While the others talk, the warrior trains himself in the use of the sword and keeps his eye on the horizon.

The warrior of light is a believer.

Because he believes in miracles, miracles begin to happen. Because he is sure that his thoughts can change his life, his life begins to change. Because he is certain that he will find love, that love appears.

Now and then, he is disappointed. Sometimes, he gets hurt.

Then he hears people say: 'He's so ingenuous!'

But the warrior knows that it is worth it. For every defeat, he has two victories in his favour.

All believers know this.

The warrior of light has learned that it is best to follow the light.

He has behaved treacherously, he has lied, he has strayed from the path, he has courted darkness. And everything was fine, as if nothing had happened.

Then an abyss suddenly opens up; you can take a thousand steps in safety, but just one step too many can put an end to everything. Then the warrior stops before he destroys himself.

When he makes that decision, he hears four comments: 'You always do the wrong thing. You're too old to change. You're no good. You don't deserve it.'

He looks up at the sky. And a voice says: 'My dear, everyone makes mistakes. You're forgiven, but I cannot force that forgiveness on you. It's your choice.'

The true warrior of light accepts that forgiveness.

The warrior of light is always trying to improve.

Every blow of his sword carries with it centuries of wisdom and meditation. Every blow needs to have the strength and skill of all the warriors of the past who, even today, continue to bless the struggle. Each movement during combat honours the movements that the previous generations tried to transmit through the Tradition.

The warrior develops the beauty of his blows.

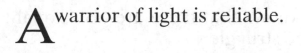

A warrior of light is reliable.

He makes a few mistakes, he sometimes thinks he is more important than he really is, but he does not lie.

When people gather round the fire, he talks to his friends, male and female. He knows that his words are stored in the memory of the Universe, like a testimony of what he thinks.

And the warrior asks himself: 'Why do I talk so much, when often I am incapable of carrying out everything I say?'

His heart replies: 'When you defend your ideas in public, you then have to make an effort to live accordingly.'

It is because he believes that he is what he says he is that the warrior ends up becoming precisely that.

The warrior knows that there are occasional pauses in the struggle.

There is no point in forcing things; he must have patience and wait for the two sides to clash again. In the silence of the battlefield, he listens to his heart beating.

He notices that he is tense, that he is afraid.

The warrior takes stock of his life; he makes sure that his sword is sharp, his heart satisfied, that faith still burns in his soul. He knows that maintenance is as important as action.

There is always something not quite right. And the warrior takes advantage of those moments when time stops to equip himself better.

A warrior knows that an angel and a devil are both competing for his sword hand.

The devil says: 'You will weaken. You will not know exactly when. You are afraid.' The angel says: 'You will weaken. You will not know exactly when. You are afraid.'

The warrior is surprised. Both angel and devil have said the same thing.

Then the devil goes on: 'Let me help you.' And the angel says: 'I will help you.'

At that moment, the warrior understands the difference. The words may be the same, but these two allies are completely different.

And he chooses the angel's hand.

Whenever the warrior draws his sword, he uses it.

It can be used to clear a path, to help someone, to fend off danger, but a sword is a capricious thing and does not like to see its blade exposed for no good reason.

That is why the warrior never makes threats. He can attack, defend himself or flee; all of these attitudes form part of combat. It is not, however, part of combat to diminish the force of a blow by talking about it.

A warrior of light is always alert to the movements of his sword. But he never forgets that the sword is watching his every move as well.

It was not made to be used by the mouth.

Sometimes evil pursues the warrior of light, and when it does, he calmly invites it into his tent.

He asks evil: 'Do you want to hurt me or use me to hurt others?'

Evil pretends not to hear. It says that it knows the darkness in the warrior's soul. It touches wounds that have not yet healed and calls for vengeance. It mentions certain tricks and subtle poisons that will help him to destroy his enemies.

The warrior of light listens. If conversation flags, he encourages evil to continue talking by asking all about its various plans.

When he has heard everything, he gets up and leaves. Evil feels so weary and empty after all this talk that it does not have the strength to follow him.

The warrior of light unwittingly takes a false step and plunges into the abyss.

Ghosts frighten him and solitude torments him. His aim had been to fight the Good Fight, and he never imagined that this would happen to him, but it did. Shrouded in darkness, he makes contact with his master.

'Master, I have fallen into the abyss,' he says. 'The waters are deep and dark.'

'Remember one thing,' replies his master. 'You do not drown simply by plunging into water, you only drown if you stay beneath the surface.'

And the warrior uses all his strength to escape from his predicament.

The warrior of light behaves like a child.

People are shocked; they have forgotten that a child needs to have fun and to play, to be slightly irreverent and to ask awkward, childish questions, to talk nonsense that not even he believes in.

And they say, horrified: 'So this is the spiritual path, is it? He's so immature!'

The warrior feels proud of such comments. And he remains in touch with God through his innocence and his joy, without ever losing sight of his mission.

The Latin root of the word 'responsibility' reveals its true meaning: the capacity to respond, to react.

A responsible warrior is one who has proved able to observe and to learn. He is even capable of being 'irresponsible'. Sometimes, he has allowed himself to be carried along by a situation, without responding or reacting.

But he always learned his lesson; he took a stance, listened to advice and was humble enough to accept help.

A responsible warrior is not someone who takes the weight of the world on his shoulders, but someone who has learned to deal with the challenges of the moment.

A warrior of light cannot always choose his battlefield.

Sometimes he is taken by surprise in the middle of battles not of his choosing, but there is no point in running away, those battles will merely follow him.

Then, at the point when conflict seems almost inevitable, the warrior talks to his opponent. Showing neither fear nor cowardice, he tries to find out why the other man wants to fight, what made him leave his village in order to seek him out to fight this duel. Without even unsheathing his sword, the warrior persuades his opponent that this is not a fight for him.

A warrior of light listens to what his opponent has to say. He only fights if absolutely necessary.

The warrior of light is terrified when it comes to making important decisions.

'This is too much for you,' says a friend. 'Go on, be brave,' says another. And so his doubts grow.

After some days of anxiety, he withdraws to the corner of his tent where he usually sits to meditate and pray. He sees himself in the future. He sees the people who will benefit or be harmed by his attitude. He does not want to cause pointless suffering, but nor does he want to abandon the path.

The warrior allows the decision to reveal itself.

If he has to say 'yes', he will say it bravely. If he has to say 'no', he will say it without a trace of cowardice.

A warrior of light accepts his Personal Legend completely.

His companions say: 'He has remarkable faith!'

For a moment, the warrior feels proud, then immediately feels ashamed of what he has heard because he does not have as much faith as he appears to have.

At that moment, his angel whispers: 'You are only an instrument of the light. There is no reason to feel proud or to feel guilty. There are only reasons to feel happy.'

And the warrior of light, aware now that he is but an instrument, feels calmer and more secure.

'Hitler may have lost the war on the battlefield, but he ended up winning something too,' says Marek Halter, 'because man in the twentieth century created the concentration camp and revived torture and taught his fellow men that it is possible to close their eyes to the misfortunes of others.'

Perhaps he is right: there are abandoned children, massacred civilians, innocent people imprisoned, lonely old people, drunks in the gutter, madmen in power.

But perhaps he isn't right at all, for there are also warriors of light.

And warriors of light never accept what is unacceptable.

The warrior of light never forgets the old saying: the good little goat doesn't bleat.

Injustices happen. Everyone finds themselves in situations they do not deserve, usually when they are unable to defend themselves. Defeat often knocks at the warrior's door.

At such times, he remains silent. He does not waste energy on words, because they can do nothing; it is best to use his strength to resist and have patience, knowing that Someone is watching, Someone who saw the unnecessary suffering and who will not accept it.

That Someone gives him what he most needs: time. Sooner or later, everything will once more work in his favour.

A warrior of light is wise; he does not talk about his defeats.

A sword may not last very long, but the warrior of light must.

That is why he never allows himself to be deceived by his own abilities and thus avoids being taken by surprise. He gives each thing the value it deserves.

Often, when the warrior is pondering grave matters, the devil whispers in his ear: 'Don't worry about that, it's not important.'

At others, when he is faced by banalities, the devil says to him: 'You should pour all your energies into resolving this situation.'

The warrior does not listen to what the devil is telling him; he is the master of his sword.

A warrior of light is always vigilant.

He does not ask anyone else for permission to wield his sword; he simply takes it in his hands. Nor does he waste time explaining his actions; faithful to God's decisions, he gives his answer in what he does.

He looks to either side of him and identifies his friends. He looks behind him and identifies his opponents. He is implacable with treachery, but he does not seek revenge; he merely drives away the enemies of his life, never fighting with them any longer than is necessary.

A warrior does not try to seem, he is.

A warrior does not keep company with those who wish to harm him. Nor is he seen in the company of those who want to 'console' him.

He avoids anyone who is only by his side in the event of a defeat: these false friends want to prove that weakness is rewarded. They always bring him bad news. They always try to destroy the warrior's confidence, all under the cloak of 'solidarity'.

When they see him wounded, they dissolve in tears, but, in their heart of hearts, they are happy because the warrior has lost a battle. They do not understand that this is part of the fight.

The true companions of a warrior are beside him always, during the difficult times and the easy times.

At the beginning of his struggle, the warrior of light stated: 'I have dreams.'

After some years, he realises that it is actually possible to reach his goal; he knows that he will be rewarded.

At that moment, he feels sad. He knows about other people's unhappiness, about the loneliness and frustration experienced by so much of humanity, and he does not believe that he deserves what he is about to receive.

His angel whispers: 'Give it all up.' The warrior kneels down and offers God his conquests.

That act of surrender forces the warrior to stop asking foolish questions and helps him to overcome his feelings of guilt.

The warrior of light has the sword in his hands.

He is the one who decides what he will do and what he will never do.

There are moments when life leads him into a crisis; he is separated from things he has always loved; it is then that the warrior reflects. He checks that he is fulfilling God's will or if he is merely acting selfishly. If this separation is really part of his path, then he accepts it without complaint.

If, however, such a separation was provoked by someone else's perverse actions, then he is implacable in his response.

The warrior possesses both force and forgiveness. He can use both with equal skill.

The warrior of light never falls into the trap of that word 'freedom'.

When his people are oppressed, freedom is a very clear concept. At such times, using sword and shield, he fights as long as he has breath and life. When contrasted with oppression, freedom is easy to understand: it is the opposite of slavery.

But sometimes the warrior hears older people saying: 'When I stop working, I will be free.' A year later, those same people are complaining: 'Life is all boring routine.' In this case, freedom is difficult to understand: it means absence of meaning.

A warrior of light is always committed. He is the slave of his dream and free to act.

A warrior of light is not constantly repeating the same struggle, especially when there are neither advances nor retreats.

If a battle is not progressing, he knows that he must sit down with the enemy and negotiate a truce; they have both practised the art of the sword, now they need to understand each other.

This is a dignified gesture, not a cowardly one. It is a balance of forces and a change of strategy.

Once the peace plans have been drawn up, the warriors return to their houses. They do not need to prove anything to anyone; they fought the Good Fight and kept the faith. Each one gave a little, thus learning the art of negotiation.

The friends of the warrior of light ask him where he draws his energy from. He says: 'From the hidden enemy.'

His friends ask who that is.

The warrior responds: 'Someone we can no longer hurt.'

It might be a boy who beat him in a childhood scrap, the girlfriend who left him when he was eleven, the teacher who said he was stupid. When he is tired, the warrior reminds himself that these enemies have still not seen his courage.

He does not consider revenge, because the hidden enemy is no longer part of his story. He thinks only of improving his skills so that his deeds will be known throughout the world and reach the ears of those who have hurt him in the past.

Yesterday's pain is the warrior of light's strength.

A warrior of light always has a second chance in life.

Like all other men and woman, he was not born knowing how to use a sword; he made many mistakes before he discovered his Personal Legend.

No warrior can sit down by the fire and tell the others: 'I always did the right thing.' Anyone who says this is lying and has not yet learned to know himself. The true warrior of light has committed injustices in the past.

But as he proceeds on his journey, he realises that the people to whom he did not behave correctly always cross his path again.

It is his chance to right the wrong he did them, and he always, unhesitatingly, seizes that chance.

A warrior is as wise as a serpent and as innocent as a dove.

When people gather to talk, he does not judge the behaviour of others; he knows that darkness uses an invisible net to spread its evil. This net catches any snippet of information floating in the air and transforms it into the intrigue and envy that infest the human soul.

Thus, everything that is said about someone reaches the ears of the enemies of that person, augmented by the dark weight of poison and malice.

For this reason, when the warrior speaks of his brother's opinions, he imagines that his brother is there present, listening to what he is saying.

The Breviary of Medieval Knights says:

'The spiritual energy of the Path uses justice and patience to prepare your spirit.

This is the Path of the Knight: a path that is at once easy and difficult, because it forces one to set aside trivial things and chance friendships. That is why, at first, many hesitate to follow it.

This is the first teaching of the Knights: you will erase everything you had written in the book of your life up until now: restlessness, uncertainty, lies. And in the place of all this you will write the word courage. By beginning the journey with that word and continuing with faith in God, you will arrive wherever you need to arrive.'

When the moment for combat approaches, the warrior of light is prepared for all eventualities.

He analyses every strategy and asks: 'What would I do if I had to fight myself?' He thus discovers his weak points.

At that moment, his opponent approaches; he comes with a bag full of promises, treaties, negotiations. He has tempting proposals and easy alternatives.

The warrior analyses each of the proposals; he also seeks agreement, but without ever losing his dignity. If he avoids combat, it will not be because he was seduced, but because he judged it to be the best strategy.

A warrior of light does not accept gifts from his enemy.

I repeat:

You can recognise a warrior of light by the look in his eye. Warriors of light are in the world, they form part of the world, and they were sent into the world without saddlebags or sandals. They are often cowardly. They do not always act correctly.

Warriors of light are wounded by the most foolish things, they worry about trivialities, they believe themselves incapable of growing. Warriors of light sometimes believe themselves unworthy of any blessing or miracle.

Warriors of light often ask themselves what they are doing here. Often they find their lives meaningless.

That is why they are warriors of light. Because they fail. Because they ask questions. Because they keep looking for a meaning. And, in the end, they will find it.

The warrior of light is now waking from his dream.

He thinks: 'I do not know how to deal with this light that is making me grow.' The light, however, does not disappear.

The warrior thinks: 'Changes must be made that I do not feel like making.'

The light remains, because 'feel' is a word full of traps.

Then the eyes and heart of the warrior begin to grow accustomed to the light. It no longer frightens him and he finally accepts his own Legend, even if this means running risks.

The warrior has been asleep for a long time. It is only natural that he should wake up very gradually.

The experienced fighter puts up with insults; he knows the strength of his fist and the skill of his blows. Confronted by an unprepared opponent, he looks deep into his eyes and conquers him without ever having to resort to a physical fight.

As the warrior learns from his spiritual master, the light of faith shines in his eyes and he does not need to prove anything to anyone. He is not bothered by his opponent's aggressive arguments which say that God is a superstition, that miracles are just tricks, that believing in angels is running away from reality.

Like the fighter, the warrior of light is aware of his own immense strength; he never fights with anyone who does not deserve the honour of combat.

The warrior of light must always remember the five rules of combat, set down by Chuan Tzu three thousand years ago:

Faith Before going into battle, you must believe in the reasons for the fight.

Companions Choose your allies and learn to fight in company, for no one ever won a war single-handed.

Time A battle in winter is different from a battle in summer; a good warrior is careful to select the right moment to begin a fight.

Space One does not fight in the same way in a mountain pass as one would on a plain. Think about your surroundings and how best to move around in them.

Strategy The best warrior is one who plans his fight.

The warrior rarely knows the result of a battle when the battle is over.

The activity of fighting will have generated an enormous amount of energy around him and there is always a moment when victory and defeat are equally possible. Time will tell who won and who lost, but he knows that, from that moment on, he can do nothing more: the fate of that battle lies in God's hands.

At such moments, the warrior of light is not concerned with results. He examines his heart and asks: 'Did I fight the Good Fight?' If the answer is 'yes', he can rest. If the answer is 'no', he takes up his sword and begins training all over again.

Each warrior of light contains within him the spark of God.

His destiny is to be with other warriors, but sometimes he will need to practise the art of the sword alone; this is why, when he is apart from his companions, he behaves like a star.

He lights up his allotted part of the Universe and tries to point out galaxies and worlds to all those who gaze up at the sky.

The warrior's persistence will soon be rewarded. Gradually, other warriors approach, and they join together to form constellations, each with their own symbols and mysteries.

Sometimes the warrior feels as if he were living two lives at once.

In one of them he is obliged to do all the things he does not want to do and to fight for ideas in which he does not believe. But there is another life, and he discovers it in his dreams, in his reading and in his encounters with people who share his ideas.

The warrior allows his two lives to draw near. 'There is a bridge that links what I do with what I would like to do,' he thinks. Slowly, his dreams take over his everyday life, and then he realises that he is ready for the thing he always wanted.

Then all that is needed is a little daring, and his two lives become one.

Write down again what I told you:

The warrior of light needs time to himself. And he uses that time for rest, contemplation and contact with the Soul of the World. Even in the midst of a battle, he manages to meditate.

Occasionally, the warrior sits down, relaxes and lets everything that is happening around him continue to happen. He looks at the world as a spectator, he does not try to add to it or take away from it, he merely surrenders unresistingly to the movement of life.

Little by little, everything that seemed complicated begins to become simple. And the warrior is glad.

The warrior of light is wary of people who think they know the path.

They are always so confident of their own ability to make decisions that they do not notice the irony with which destiny writes each life, and they always complain when the inevitable knocks at the door.

The warrior of light has dreams. His dreams carry him forward. But he never makes the mistake of thinking that the way is broad and the gate wide. He knows that the Universe functions in the same way as alchemy: *solve et coagula* said the masters—'Concentrate and disperse your energies according to the situation.'

There are moments when one should act and moments when one should accept. The warrior knows how to distinguish between these moments.

The warrior of light, once he has learned how to use a sword, discovers that his equipment is still incomplete—he needs armour.

He sets off in search of this armour and he listens to the advice of various salesmen.

'Use the breastplate of solitude,' says one.

'Use the shield of cynicism', says another.

'The best armour is not to get involved in anything,' says a third.

The warrior, however, ignores them. He calmly goes to his sacred place and puts on the indestructible cloak of faith.

Faith parries all blows. Faith transforms poison into crystal clear water.

'I always believe everything anyone tells me and I'm always disappointed,' his companion says.

It is important to trust people; a warrior of light is not afraid of disappointments because he knows the power of his sword and the strength of his love.

However, he imposes certain limits: it is one thing to accept God's signs and to know that the angels use the mouths of other people to give us advice. It is quite another to be incapable of making decisions and to be always looking for ways of letting others tell us what we should do.

A warrior trusts other people because, first and foremost, he trusts himself.

The warrior of light views life with tenderness and determination.

He stands before a mystery, whose solution he will one day find. Every so often, he says to himself: 'This life is absolutely insane.'

He is right. In surrendering to the miracle of the everyday, he notices that he cannot always foresee the consequences of his actions. Sometimes he acts without even knowing that he is doing so, he saves someone without even knowing he is saving them, he suffers without even knowing why he is sad.

Yes, life is insane. But the great wisdom of the warrior lies in choosing his insanity wisely.

The warrior of light studies the two columns on either side of the door he is trying to open.

One is called Fear and the other is called Desire. The warrior looks at the column of Fear and on it is written: 'You are entering a dangerous, unfamiliar world where everything you have learned up until now will prove useless.'

The warrior looks at the column of Desire and on it is written: 'You are about to leave a familiar world wherein are stored all the things you ever wanted and for which you struggled long and hard.'

The warrior smiles because nothing frightens him and nothing holds him. With the confidence of one who knows what he wants, he opens the door.

A warrior of light practises a powerful exercise for inner growth: he pays attention to the things he does automatically, such as breathing, blinking, or noticing the things around him.

He does this when he feels confused, and in this way he frees himself from tensions and allows his intuition to work more freely, without interference from his fears and desires. Certain problems that appeared to be insoluble are resolved, certain sorrows from which he thought he would never recover vanish naturally.

He uses this technique whenever he is faced with a difficult situation.

The warrior of light hears comments like: 'There are certain things I'd rather not talk about because people are so envious.'

When he hears this, the warrior laughs. Envy cannot harm you, if you don't let it. Envy is part of life and everyone should learn to deal with it.

However, he rarely discusses his plans. And sometimes people believe this is because he is afraid of envy.

But he knows that whenever he talks about a dream, he uses a little bit of the energy from that dream in order to do so. And by talking, he runs the risk of spending all the energy he needs to put the dream into action.

A warrior of light knows the power of words.

The warrior of light knows the value of persistence and of courage.

Often, during combat, he receives blows that he was not expecting. And he realises that, during war, his enemy is bound to win some of the battles. When this happens, he weeps bitter tears and rests in order to recover his energies a little. But he immediately resumes his battle for his dreams.

The longer he remains away, the more likely he is to feel weak, fearful and intimidated. When a horseman falls off his horse, if he does not remount immediately, he will never have the courage to do so again.

A warrior knows when a battle is worth fighting.

He bases his decisions on inspiration and faith. He nevertheless meets people who ask him to fight battles that are not his own, on battlefields that he does not know or which do not interest him. They want to involve the warrior of light in contests that are important to them, but not to him.

Often these are people close to the warrior of light, people who love him and trust in his strength and who want him to ease their anxieties in some way.

At such moments, he smiles and makes it clear to them that he loves them, but he does not take up the challenge.

A true warrior of light always chooses his own battlefield.

The warrior of light knows how to lose.

He does not treat defeat as if it were a matter of indifference to him, saying things like 'Oh, it doesn't matter' or 'To be honest, I didn't really want it that much', He accepts defeat as defeat and does not try to make a victory out of it.

Painful wounds, the indifference of friends, the loneliness of losing—all leave a bitter taste. But at these times, he says to himself: 'I fought for something and did not succeed. I lost the first battle.'

These words give him renewed strength. He knows that no one wins all the time and he knows how to distinguish his successes from his failures.

When somebody wants something, the whole Universe conspires in their favour. The warrior of light knows this.

For this reason, he takes great care with his thoughts. Hidden beneath a whole series of good intentions lie feelings that no one dares confess to himself: vengeance, self-destruction, guilt, fear of winning, a macabre joy at other people's tragedies.

The Universe does not judge; it conspires in favour of what we want. That is why the warrior has the courage to look into the dark places of his soul in order to ensure that he is not asking for the wrong things.

And he is always very careful about what he thinks.

Jesus said: 'Let your yea be yea; and your nay, nay.' When the warrior takes on a commitment, he keeps his word.

Those who make promises they do not keep lose their self-respect and feel ashamed of their actions. These people spend their lives in constant flight; they expend far more energy on coming up with a series of excuses to unsay what they said than the warrior of light does in honouring his commitments.

Sometimes he too takes on a foolish commitment which will in some way harm him. He does not repeat this mistake, but he nevertheless keeps his word and pays the price for his own impulsiveness.

When he wins a battle, the warrior celebrates.

This victory has cost him anxious moments, nights racked with doubt, endless days of waiting. Since ancient times, celebrating a triumph has been part of the ritual of life itself: celebration is a rite of passage.

His companions see the warrior of light's joy and think: 'Why is he doing that? He might be disappointed in his next battle. He might draw down on himself the wrath of his enemy.'

But the warrior knows why he is celebrating. He is savouring the best gift that victory can bring: confidence.

He celebrates yesterday's victory in order to gain more strength for tomorrow's battle.

One day, for no apparent reason, the warrior realises that he does not feel the same enthusiasm for the fight that he used to.

He continues to do what he has always done, but every gesture seems meaningless. At such a time, he has only one choice: to continue fighting the Good Fight. He says his prayers out of duty or fear or whatever, but he does not abandon the path.

He knows that the angel of the One who inspires him has simply wandered off somewhere. The warrior keeps his attention focused on the battle and he perseveres, even when everything seems utterly pointless. The angel will soon return and the merest flutter of his wings will restore the warrior's joy to him.

A warrior of light shares with others what he knows of the path.

Anyone who gives help also receives help and needs to teach what he has learned. That is why he sits by the fire and recounts his day on the battlefield.

A friend whispers: 'Why talk so openly about your strategy? Don't you realise that, by doing so, you run the risk of sharing your conquests with others?'

The warrior merely smiles and says nothing. He knows that if, at the end of his journey, he arrives to find an empty paradise, his struggle will have been a waste of time.

The warrior of light has learned that God uses solitude to teach us how to live with other people.

He uses rage to show us the infinite value of peace. He uses boredom to underline the importance of adventure and spontaneity.

God uses silence to teach us to use words responsibly. He uses tiredness so that we can understand the value of waking up. He uses illness to underline the blessing of good health.

God uses fire to teach us about water. He uses earth so that we can understand the value of air. He uses death to show us the importance of life.

The warrior of light gives before he is asked.

Seeing this, some of his companions say: 'If someone wants something, they'll ask for it.'

But the warrior knows that there are many people who simply cannot bring themselves to ask for help. Alongside him live people with such fragile hearts that love becomes a sickness; they are starving for affection and yet are ashamed to show it.

The warrior gathers these people round the fire, he tells stories, shares his food, gets drunk with them. The following day, everyone feels better.

Those who look on other people's misery with indifference are the most miserable of all.

If the strings of an instrument are always taut, they go out of tune.

Warriors who spend all their time training lose their spontaneity in battle. Horses that are always jumping fences end up breaking a leg. Bows that are bent all day no longer shoot arrows with the same force.

That is why, even if he is not in the mood, the warrior of light tries to enjoy the small everyday things of life.

The warrior of light listens to Lao Tzu when he says that we should let go of the idea of days and hours in order to pay more attention to the moment.

Only in this way can the warrior resolve certain problems before they occur; by focusing on the small things, he manages to avoid larger calamities.

But thinking about the small things is not the same as thinking small. Over-anxiety ultimately banishes every trace of joy from life.

The warrior knows that a great dream is made up of many different things, just as the light from the sun is the sum of its millions of rays.

There are times when the warrior's path becomes merely routine. Then he applies the teaching of Rabbi Nachman of Breslov:

'If you cannot meditate, you should repeat one simple word, because this is good for the soul. Do not say anything else, just repeat that word over and over, innumerable times. Finally, it will lose all meaning, but take on an entirely new significance. God will open the doors and you will find yourself using that simple word to say everything that you wanted to say.'

When he is forced to perform the same task several times, the warrior uses this tactic and transforms work into prayer.

A warrior of light has no 'certainties', he just has a path to follow, a path to which he tries to adapt depending on the season.

During battles that take place in summer he does not use the same equipment and techniques that he would use during battles that take place in winter. By being flexible, he no longer judges the world on the basis of 'right' and 'wrong', but on the basis of 'the most appropriate attitude for that particular moment'.

He knows that his companions also have to adapt and is not surprised when they change their attitude. He gives each one the necessary time to justify his actions.

But when it comes to treachery, he is implacable.

A warrior sits around the fire with his friends.

They spend hours criticising each other, but they end the night sleeping in the same tent, having forgotten all the insults that were bandied about. Occasionally, a new member joins the group. Because he does not yet share a common history, he shows only his good qualities, and some see in him a master.

But the warrior of light never compares him with his old companions in battle. He makes the stranger welcome, but he will not trust him until he knows his defects too.

A warrior of light does not go into battle without knowing the limitations of his ally.

The warrior knows an old saying: 'If regrets could kill . . .'

And he knows that regrets can kill; they slowly eat away at the soul of someone who has done something wrong and they lead eventually to self-destruction.

The warrior does not want to die like that. When he acts perversely or maliciously—because he is a man of many faults—he is never too ashamed to ask forgiveness.

If possible, he does his best to repair the wrong he has done. If the injured party is dead, then he does some good turn to a stranger and offers up that deed to the soul that he wounded.

A warrior of light has no regrets, because regrets can kill. He humbles himself and undoes the wrong he has done.

All warriors of light have heard their mothers say: 'My son wasn't thinking straight when he did that; deep down, he's a very good person.'

Although he respects his mother, he knows that this is not true. He does not waste his time blaming himself for his rash actions nor does he spend his life forgiving himself for all the wrong he has done—doing that would never set him back on the right path.

He uses common sense to judge not the intentions of an action but its consequences. He takes responsibility for everything he does, even if he has to pay a high price for his mistake.

As the old Arabic proverb says: 'God judges a tree by its fruits and not by its roots.'

Before making any important decision—declaring a war, moving with his companions to another plain, choosing a field in which to sow seed—the warrior asks himself: 'How will this affect the fifth generation of my descendants?'

A warrior knows that everything a person does has enduring consequences and he needs to understand what kind of world he is leaving behind for that fifth generation.

'It's just a storm in a teacup,' someone says to the warrior of light.

But he never exaggerates his difficulties and always tries to remain calm.

And he never judges someone else's suffering.

A small detail—which does not affect him in the least—could serve to ignite the storm brewing in his brother's soul. The warrior respects the suffering of others and does not try to compare it with his own.

The cup of suffering is not the same size for everyone.

'The most important quality on the spiritual path is courage,' said Gandhi.

The world seems threatening and dangerous to cowards. They seek the false security of a life with no major challenges and arm themselves to the teeth in order to defend what they think they possess. Cowards end up making the bars of their own prison.

The warrior of light projects his thoughts beyond the horizon. He knows that if he does not do anything for the world, no one else will.

So he fights the Good Fight and he helps others, even though he does not quite understand why.

The warrior of light pays close attention to a text that the Soul of the World transmitted to Chico Xavier:

'When you have managed to overcome grave problems in a relationship, do not spend time remembering the difficult times, concentrate on the joy of having passed yet another of life's tests. When you emerge from a long period of medical treatment, do not brood on the suffering you endured, think instead of God's blessing that allowed you to be cured.

'Carry in your memory, for the rest of your life, the good things that came out of those difficulties. They will serve as a proof of your abilities and will give you confidence when you are faced by other obstacles.'

The warrior of light concentrates on the small miracles of daily life.

He is capable of seeing what is beautiful because he carries beauty within himself, for the world is a mirror and gives back to each man the reflection of his own face. The warrior knows his faults and limitations, but he does all he can to maintain his good humour in moments of crisis.

The world is, after all, doing its best to help him, even though everything around him seems to be saying the opposite.

There is such a thing as emotional rubbish; it is produced in the factories of the mind. It consists of pain that has long since passed and is no longer useful. It consists of precautions that were important in the past, but that serve no purpose in the present.

The warrior has memories too, but he learns how to separate the useful from the unnecessary; he disposes of his emotional rubbish.

A companion says: 'But that's part of my history. Why should I jettison feelings that marked my very existence?'

The warrior smiles, but he does not try to feel things that he no longer feels. He is changing and he wants his feelings to keep pace with him.

When the master sees that the warrior is depressed, he says:

'You are not what you seem to be in these moments of sadness. You are better than that.

'Many have left—for reasons we will never understand—but you are still here. Why did God carry off all those amazing people and leave you?

'By now, millions of people will have given up. They don't get angry, they don't weep, they don't do anything; they merely wait for time to pass. They have lost the ability to react.

'You, however, are sad. That proves that your soul is still alive.'

Sometimes, in the middle of an apparently endless battle, the warrior has an idea and he manages to triumph in a matter of seconds.

Then he thinks: 'Why did I labour for so long over a battle that could have been resolved with only half the energy I spent on it?'

The truth is that all problems seem very simple once they have been resolved. The great victory, which appears so simple today, was the result of a series of small victories that went unnoticed.

Then the warrior understands what happened and he sleeps easy. Far from blaming himself for having taken so long to arrive, he is simply glad to know that he did arrive in the end.

There are two types of prayer.

In the first type, the person asks for certain things to happen and attempts to tell God what he should do. This does not allow the Creator either time or space in which to act. God—who knows perfectly well what is best for each of us—will continue to do as he sees fit. And the person praying is left with the impression that his prayer went unanswered.

In the second type, the person may not understand the Almighty's intentions, but he allows his life to develop according to his Creator's plans. He asks to be spared suffering, he asks for joy in the Good Fight, but he never forgets to add: 'Thy will be done'.

This is how the warrior of light chooses to pray.

The warrior knows that the most important words in all languages are the small words.

Yes. Love. God.

They are words that are easy enough to say and which fill vast empty spaces.

There is, however, one word—another small word—that many people have great difficulty in saying: no.

Someone who never says 'no', thinks of himself as generous, understanding, polite, because 'no' is thought of as being nasty, selfish, unspiritual.

The warrior does not fall into this trap. There are times when, in saying 'yes' to others, he is actually saying 'no' to himself.

That is why he never says 'yes' with his lips if, in his heart, he is saying 'no'.

First: God is sacrifice. Suffer in this life and you will be happy in the next.

Second: People who have fun are childish. Remain tense at all times.

Third: Other people know what is best for us because they have more experience.

Fourth: Our duty is to make other people happy. We must please them even if that means making major sacrifices.

Fifth: We must not drink from the cup of happiness; we might get to like it and we won't always have it in our hands.

Sixth: We must accept all punishments. We are guilty.

Seventh: Fear is a warning. We don't want to take any risks.

These are the commandments that no warrior of light can obey.

A very large group of people is standing in the middle of the road, barring the way into Paradise.

The puritan asks: 'What are these sinners doing here?'

And the moralist bawls: 'The prostitute wants to join the feast!'

The guardian of social values yells: 'How can the adulteress be forgiven when she has sinned?'

The penitent rends his clothes: 'Why cure a blind man if all he cares about is his illness and when he doesn't even say thank you?'

The ascetic protests: 'You let that woman pour expensive oil on your hair! Why didn't she sell it instead to buy food?'

Smiling, Jesus holds the door open. And the warriors of light go in, despite the hysterical shouting.

The opponent is wise.

Whenever he can, he makes use of the easiest and most effective of his weapons: gossip. It doesn't take much effort to use it because others do the work for him. A few misdirected words can destroy months of dedication, years spent in search of harmony.

The warrior of light is often the victim of this trick. He does not know where the blow came from and cannot prove that the gossip is false. Gossip does not allow him the right to defend himself: it condemns without a trial.

When this happens, he puts up with the consequences and the undeserved punishment, for, as he well knows, words are powerful. But he suffers in silence and never uses the same weapon to hit back at his opponent.

The warrior of light is not a coward.

'You can give a fool a thousand intellects, but the only one he will want is yours,' says an Arabic proverb. When the warrior of light starts planting his garden, he notices that his neighbour is there, spying. He likes to give advice on when to sow actions, when to fertilise thoughts and water conquests.

If he listens to what his neighbour is saying, he will end up creating something that is not his; the garden he is tending will be his neighbour's idea.

But a true warrior of light knows that every garden has its own mysteries, which only the patient hand of the gardener can unravel. That is why he prefers to concentrate on the sun, the rain and the seasons.

He knows that the fool who gives advice about someone else's garden is not tending his own plants.

In order to fight, you must keep your eyes open and have faithful companions by your side.

It can happen that someone who was fighting alongside the warrior of light suddenly becomes his opponent instead.

The warrior's first reaction is hatred, but he knows that a blind combatant is lost in the midst of battle.

And so he tries to see the good things that his former ally did during the time in which they lived side by side; he tries to understand what led to that sudden change of attitude, what wounds he had accumulated in his soul. He tries to discover what made one of them abandon their dialogue.

No one is entirely good or evil; that is what the warrior thinks when he sees that he has a new opponent.

A warrior knows that the ends do not justify the means.

Because there are no ends, there are only means. Life carries him from unknown to unknown. Each moment is filled with this thrilling mystery: the warrior does not know where he came from nor where he is going.

But he is not here by chance. And he is overjoyed by surprises and excited by landscapes that he has never seen before. He often feels afraid, but that is normal in a warrior.

If he thinks only of the goal, he will not be able to pay attention to the signs along the way. If he concentrates only on one question, he will miss the answers that are there beside him.

That is why the warrior submits.

The warrior knows about the 'waterfall effect'.

He has often seen someone mistreating another person who lacks the courage to respond. Then, out of cowardice and resentment, that person vents his anger on someone weaker than himself, who takes it out on someone else, in a veritable torrent of misery. No one knows the consequences of his own cruelty.

That is why the warrior is careful in his use of the sword and only accepts an opponent who is worthy of him. In moments of rage, he punches a rock and bruises his hand.

The hand will heal eventually, but the child who got beaten because his father lost a battle will bear the marks for the rest of his life.

When the order to move on comes, the warrior looks at all the friends he has made during the time that he followed the path. He taught some to hear the bells of a drowned temple, he told others stories around the fire.

His heart is sad, but he knows that his sword is sacred and that he must obey the orders of the One to whom he offered up his struggle.

Then the warrior thanks his travelling companions, takes a deep breath and continues on, laden with memories of an unforgettable journey.

EPILOGUE

It was dark by the time she finished speaking. The two of them sat watching the moon rising.

'Many of the things you told me contradict each other,' he said.

She got up.

'Goodbye,' she said. 'You knew that the bells at the bottom of the sea were not just a legend, but you could only hear them when you realised that the wind, the seagulls and the sound of the palm fronds were all part of the pealing of the bells.

In just the same way, the warrior of light knows that everything around him—his victories, his defeats, his enthusiasm and his despondency—form part of his Good Fight. And he will know which strategy to use when he needs it. A warrior does not try to be coherent; he has learned to live with his contradictions.'

'Who are you?' he asked.

But the woman was already moving off, walking over the waves towards the rising moon.